HAL•LEONARD

UKULELE
PLAY-ALONG

AUDIO
ACCESS
INCLUDED

PLAYBACK+
Speed • Pitch • Balance • Loop

Classical THEMES
Play 8 of Your Favorite Pieces with Professional Audio Tracks

To access audio visit:
www.halleonard.com/mylibrary

Enter Code
7135-8212-6629-8612

Ukulele by Mike Butzen

ISBN 978-1-4803-9135-2

HAL•LEONARD®
CORPORATION
7777 W. BLUEMOUND RD. P.O. BOX 13819 MILWAUKEE, WI 53213

In Australia Contact:
Hal Leonard Australia Pty. Ltd.
4 Lentara Court
Cheltenham, Victoria, 3192 Australia
Email: ausadmin@halleonard.com.au

Visit Hal Leonard Online at
www.halleonard.com

CONTENTS

Blue Danube Waltz

By Johann Strauss, Jr.

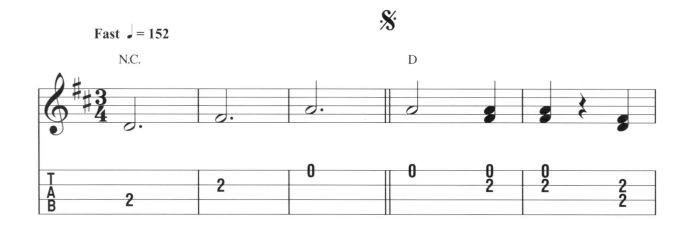

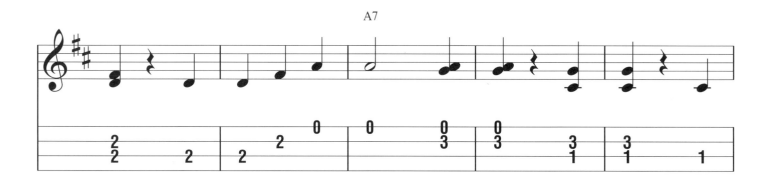

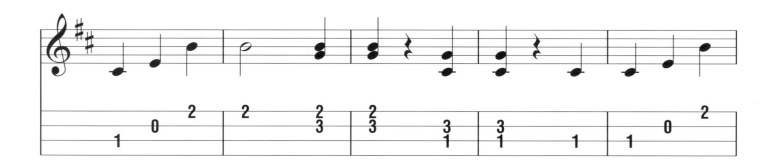

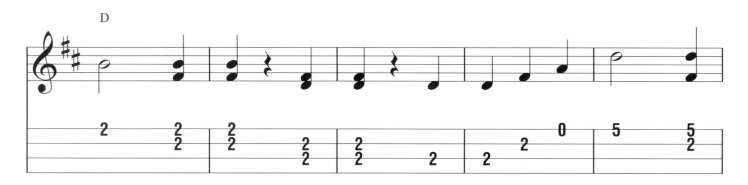

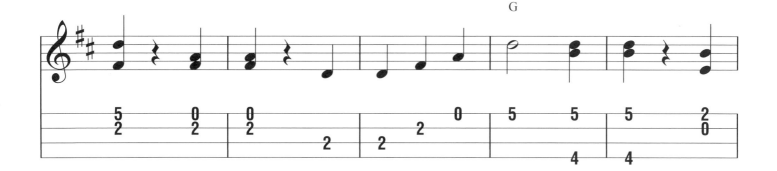

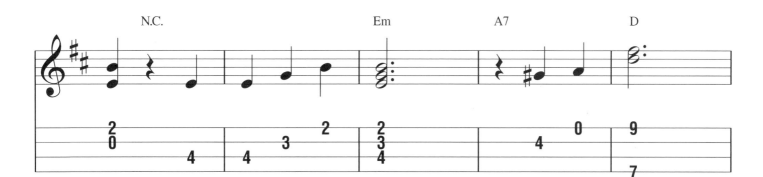

To Coda ⊕

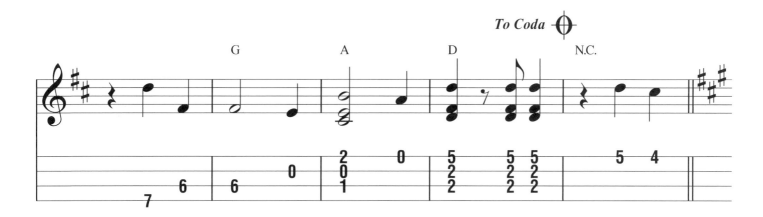

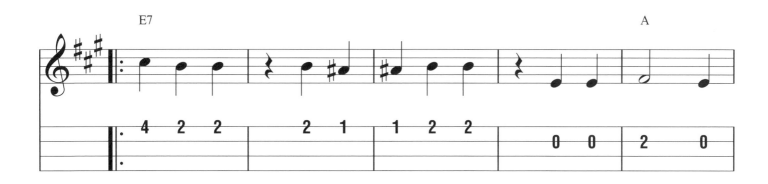

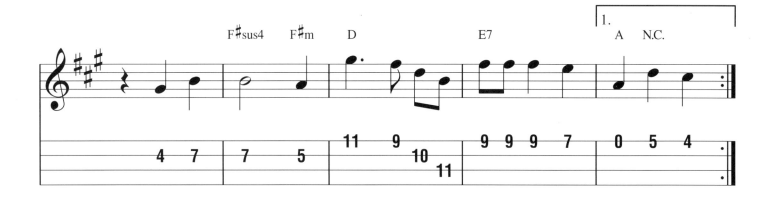

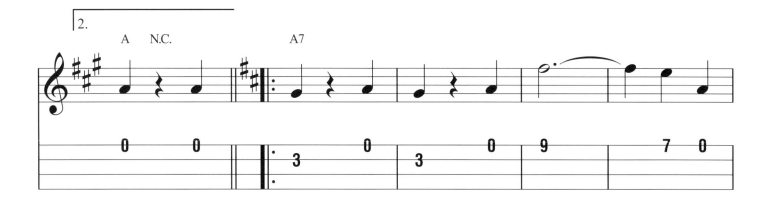

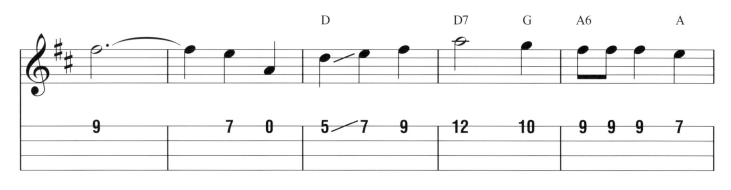

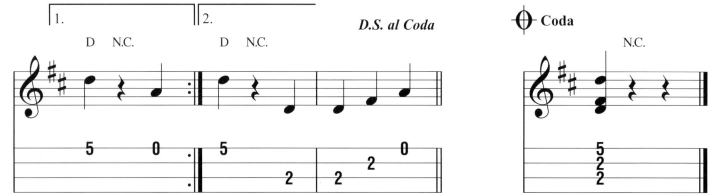

In the Hall of the Mountain King

from PEER GYNT

By Edvard Grieg

Moderately ♩ = 104

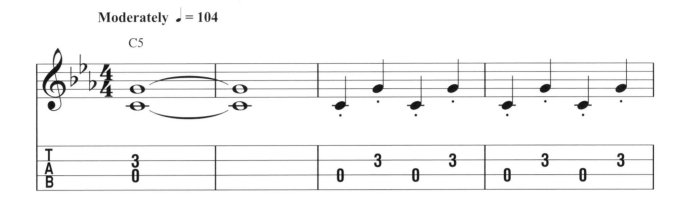

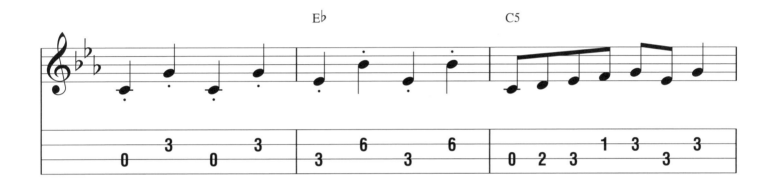

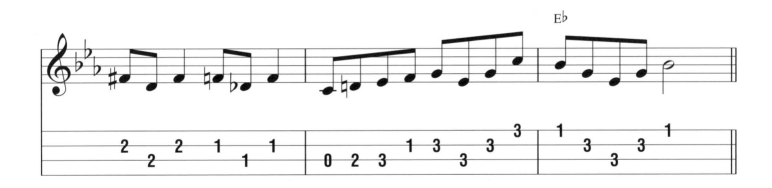

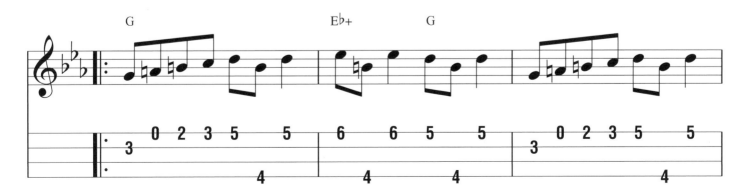

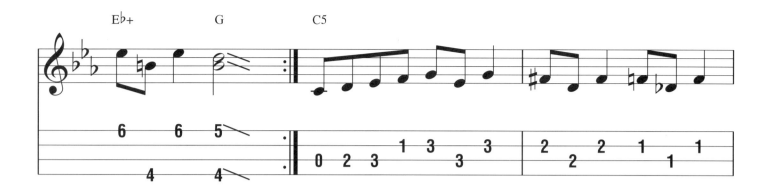

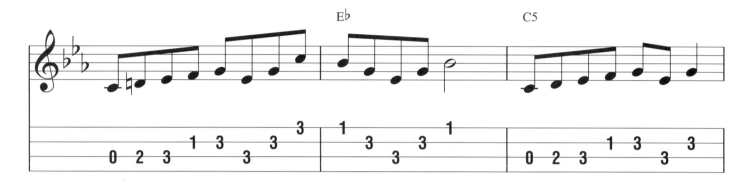

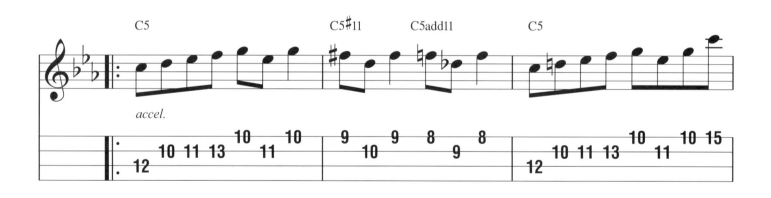

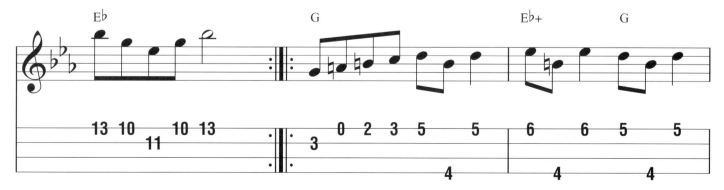

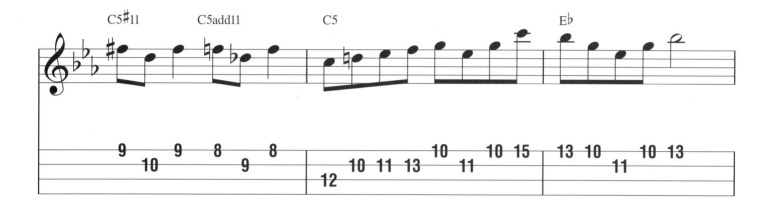

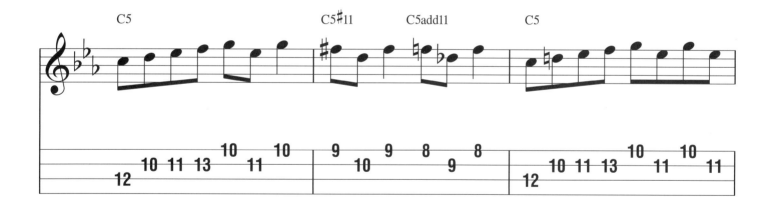

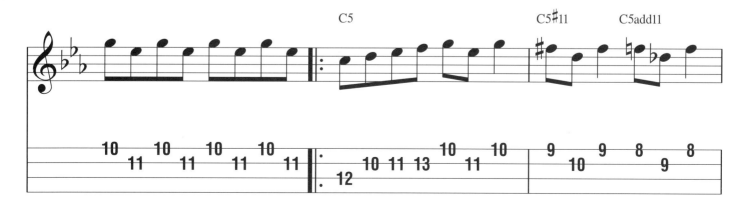

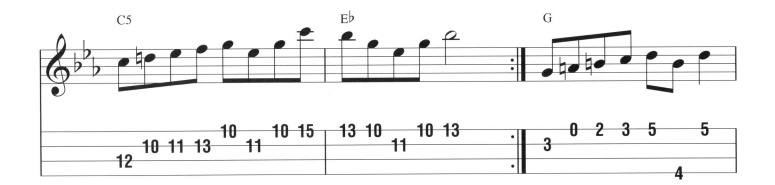

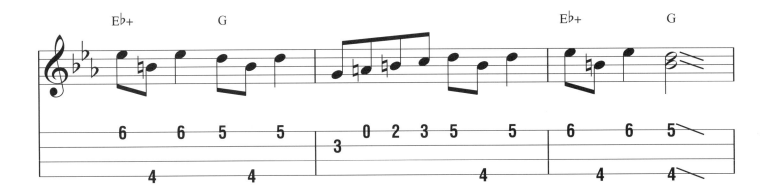

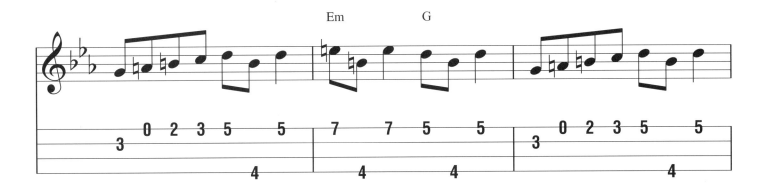

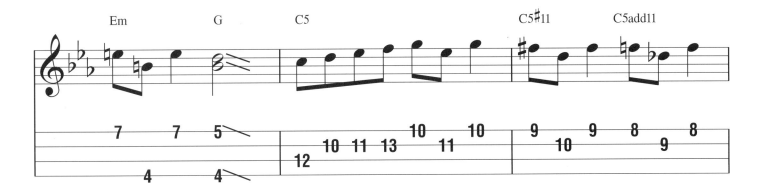

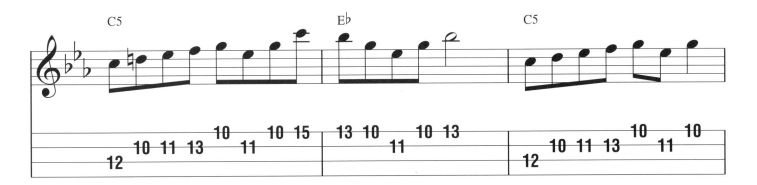

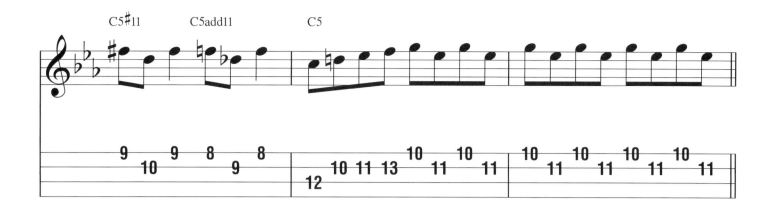

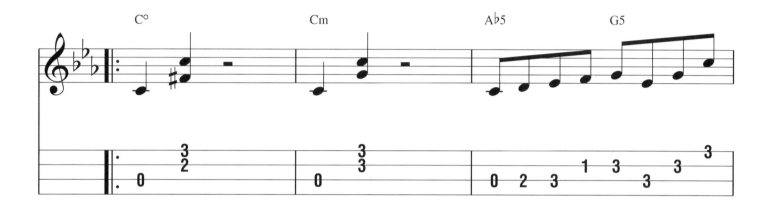

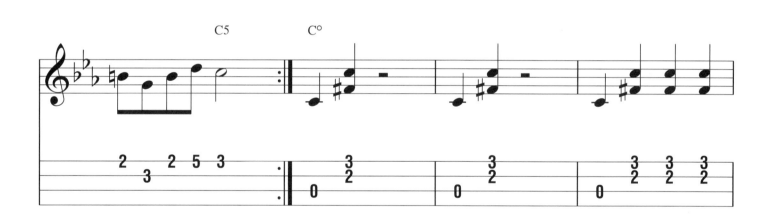

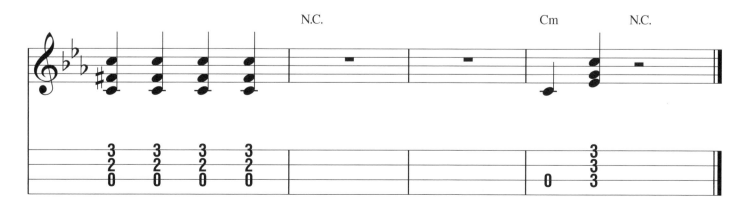

Eine Kleine Nachtmusik
("Serenade")
First Movement Excerpt
By Wolfgang Amadeus Mozart

Moderately ♩ = 124

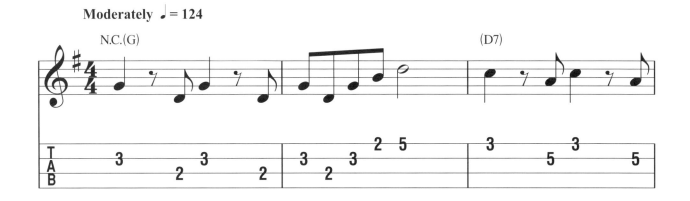

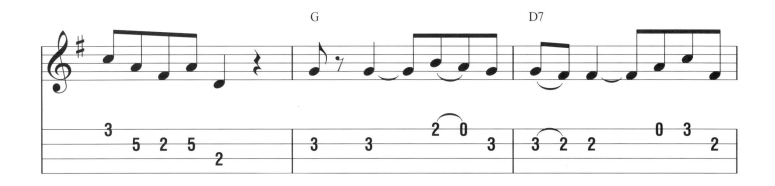

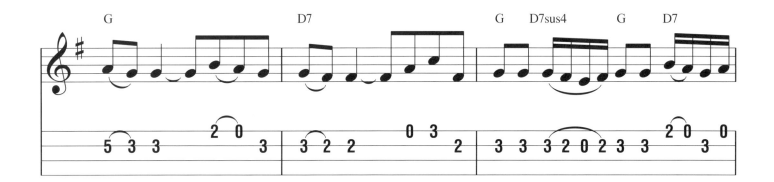

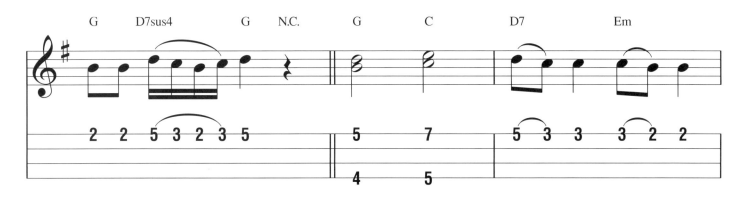

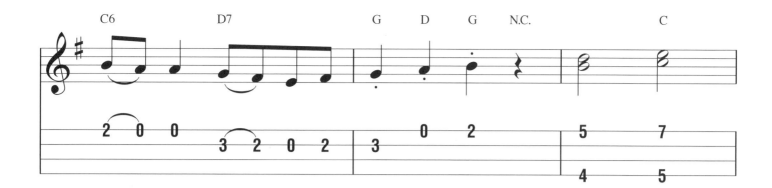

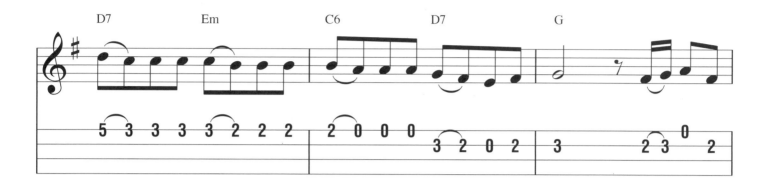

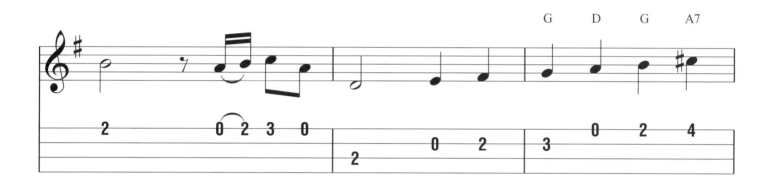

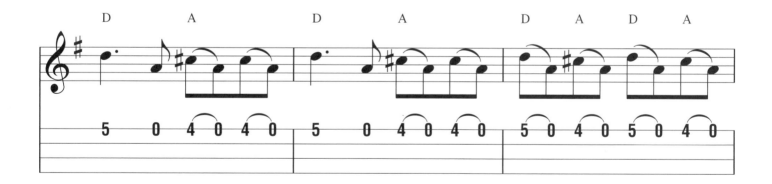

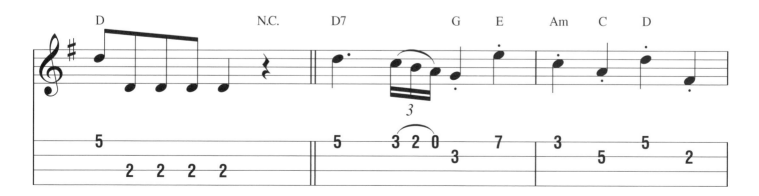

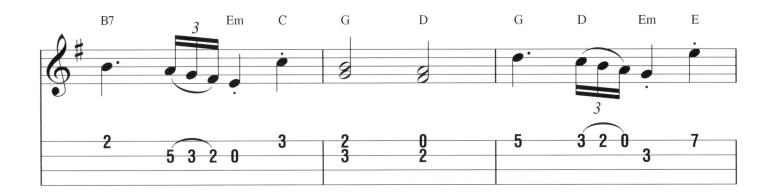

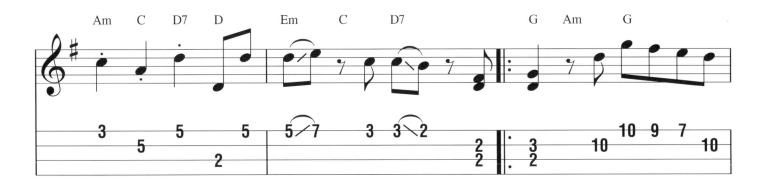

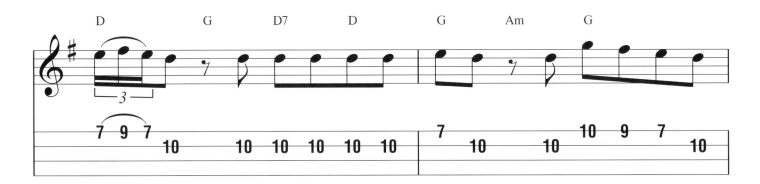

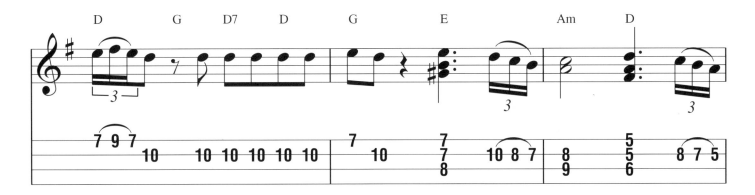

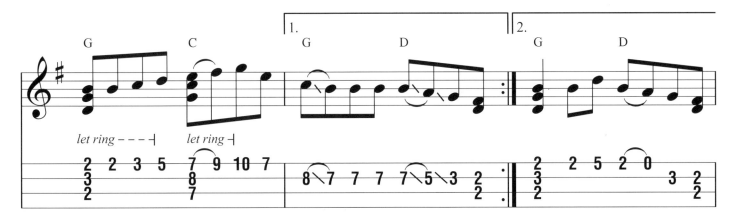

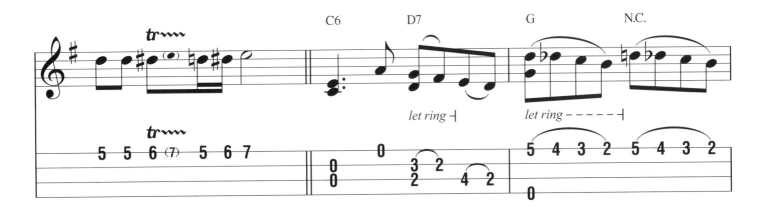

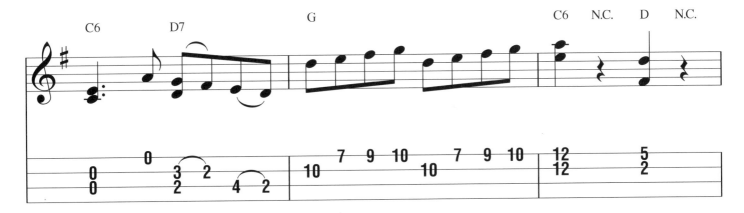

Für Elise

By Ludwig van Beethoven

Moderately ♩ = 124

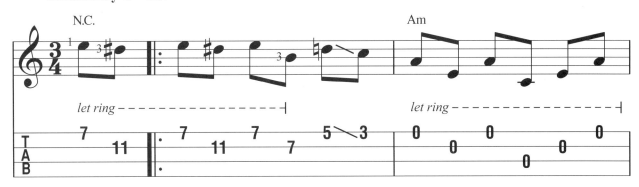

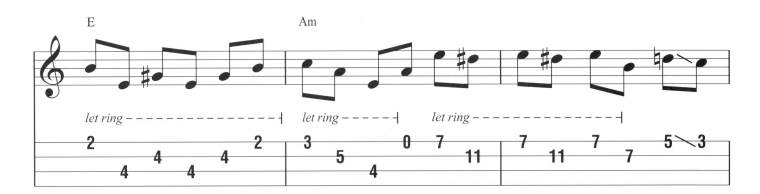

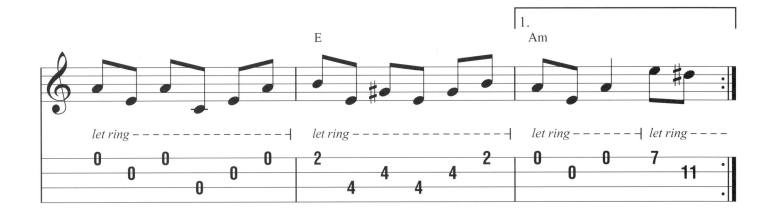

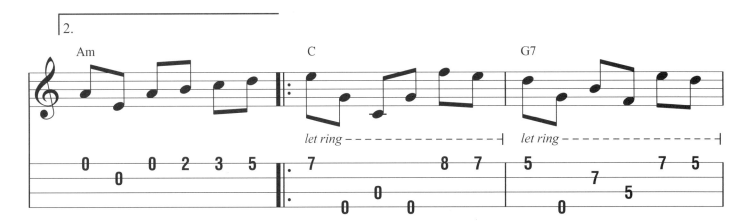

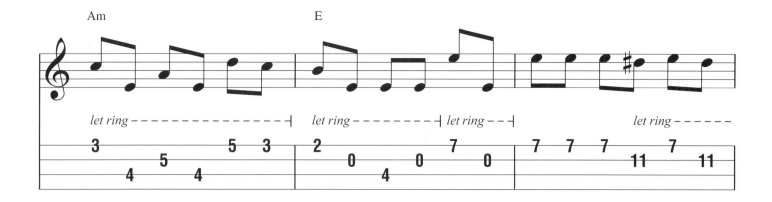

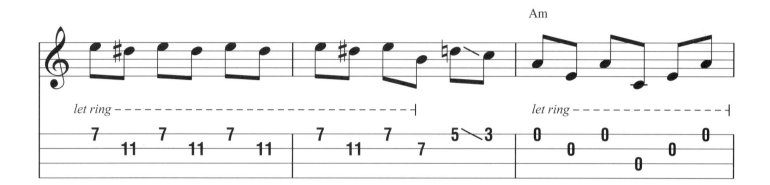

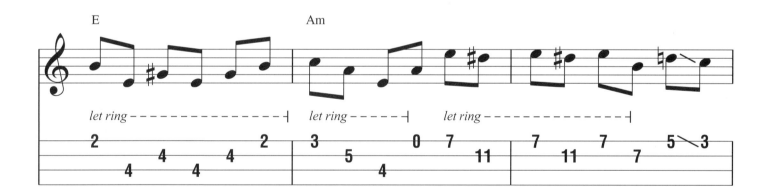

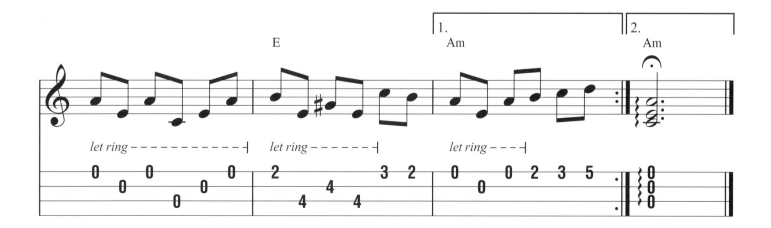

Humoresque

By Antonín Dvořák

Moderately ♩ = 112

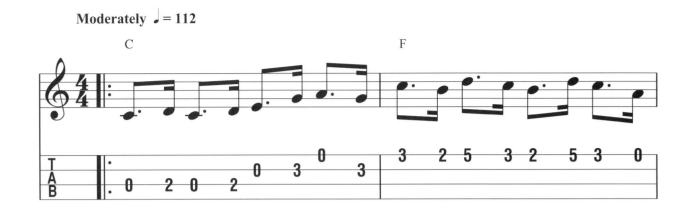

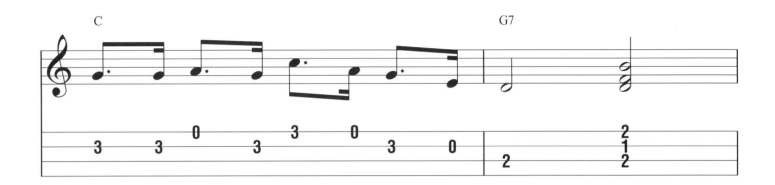

3rd time, To Coda ⊕

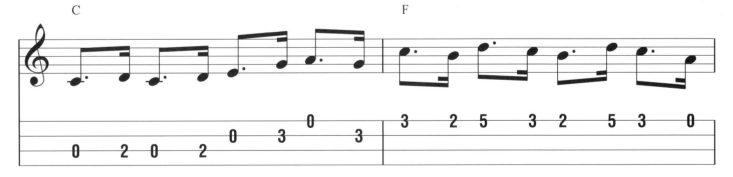

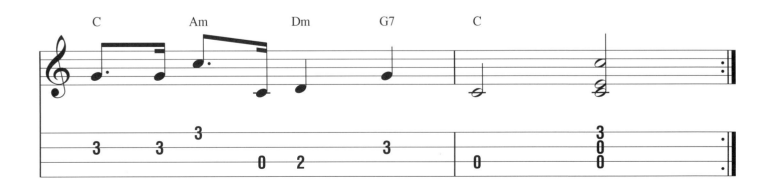

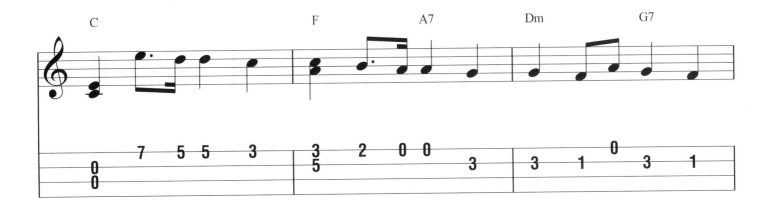

D.C. al Coda

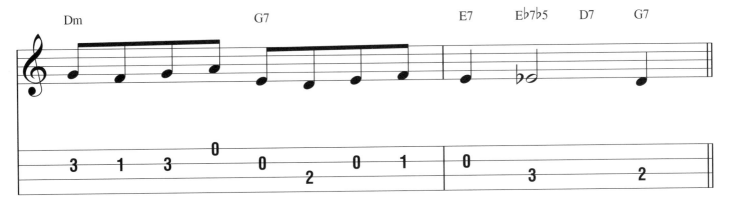

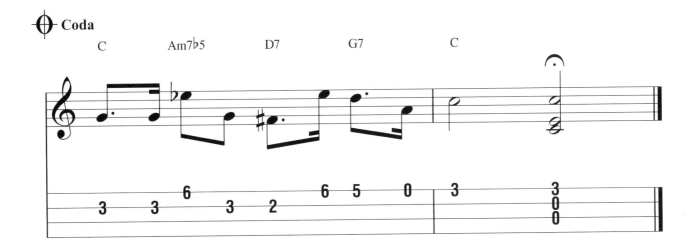

La donna è mobile

from RIGOLETTO

By Giuseppe Verdi

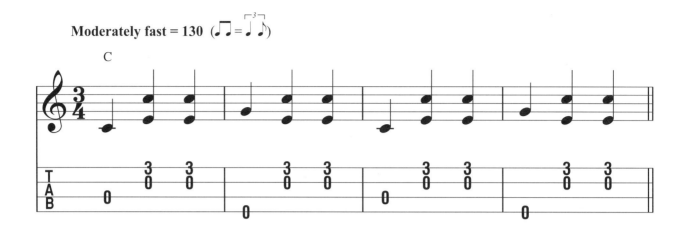

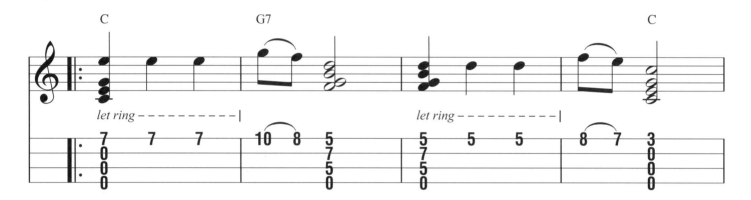

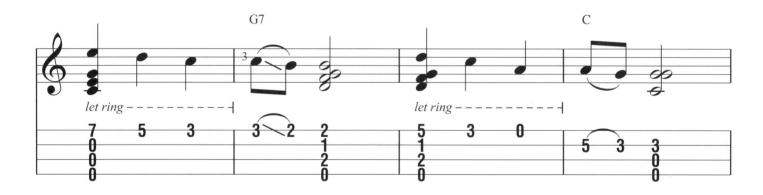

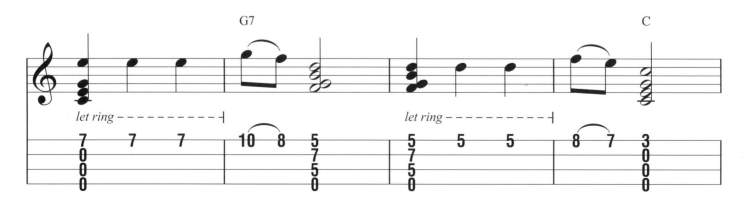

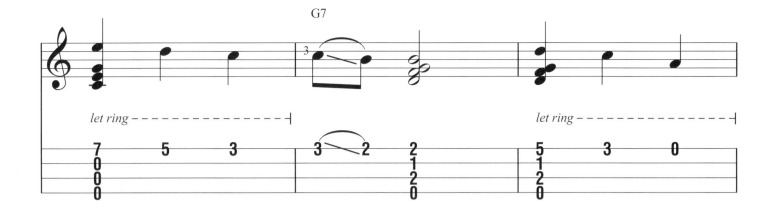

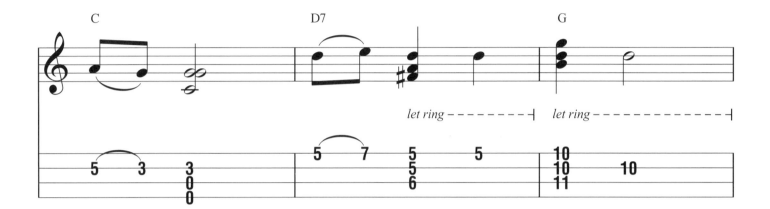

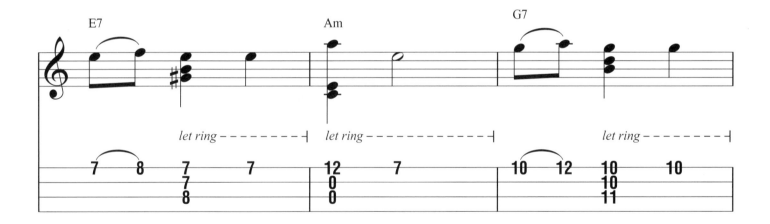

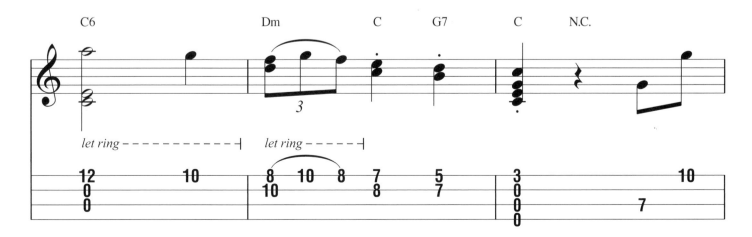

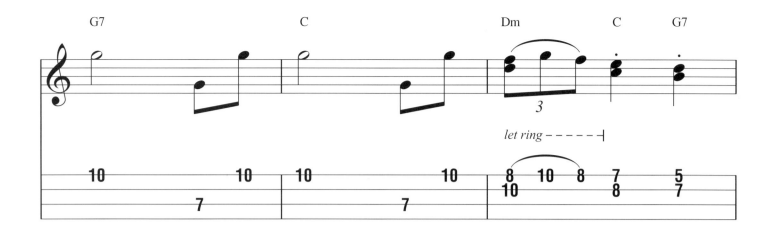

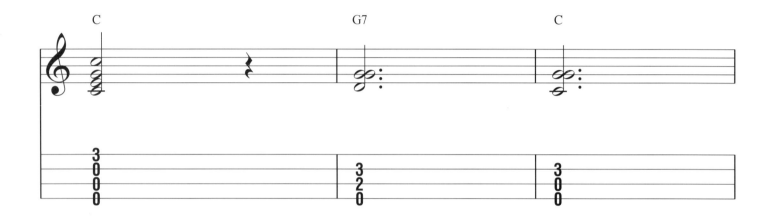

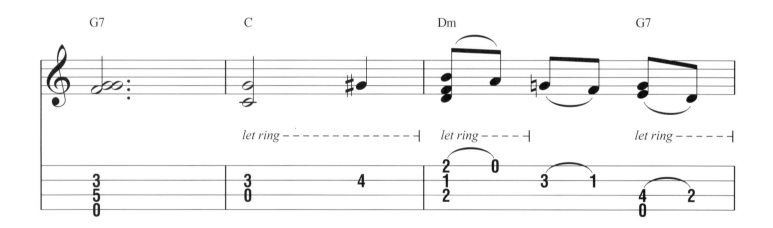

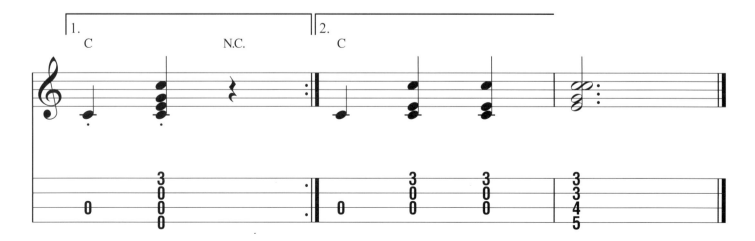

The Merry Widow Waltz

from THE MERRY WIDOW

Words by Adrian Ross
Music by Franz Lehar

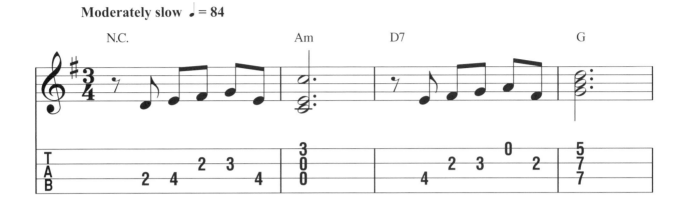

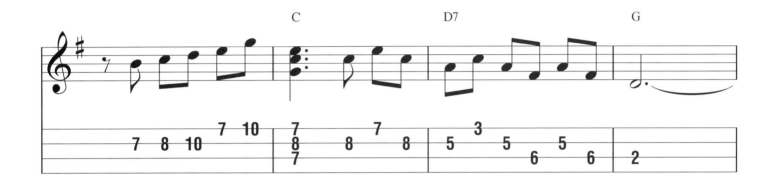

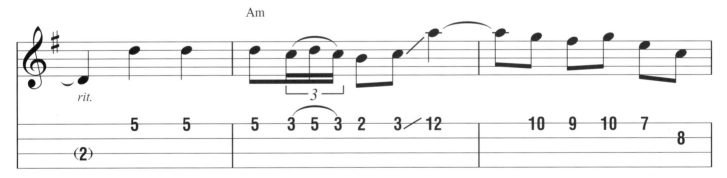

Faster ♩ = 126

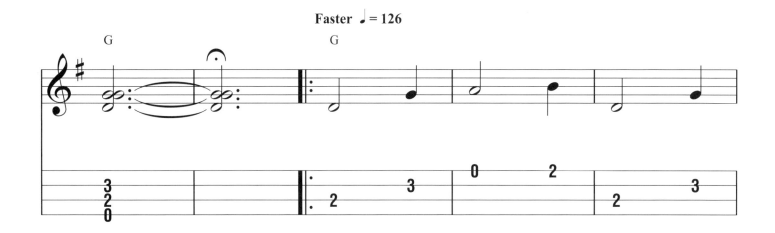

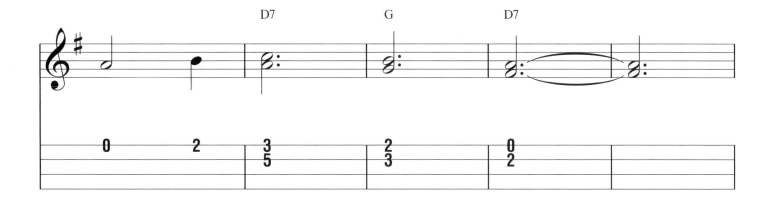

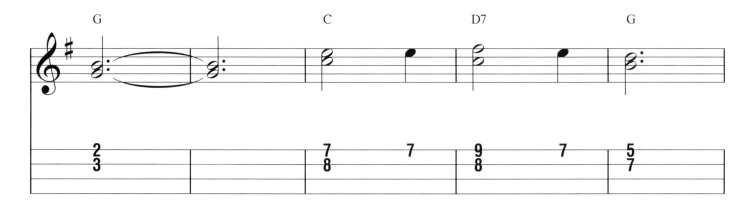

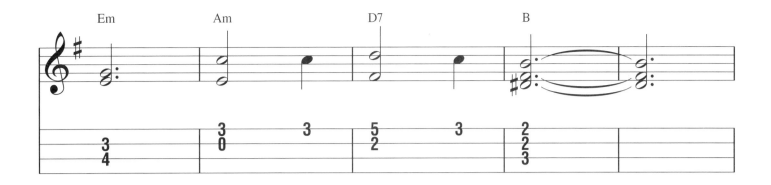

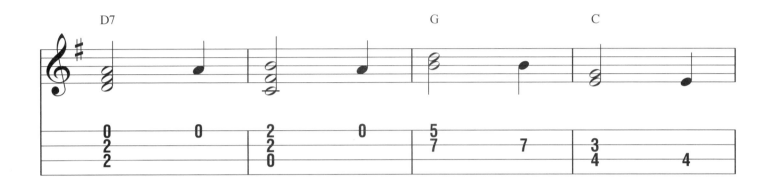

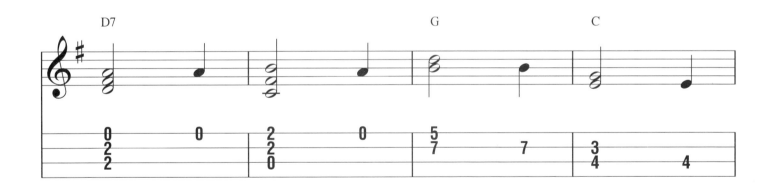

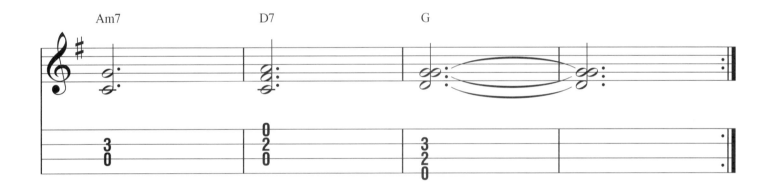

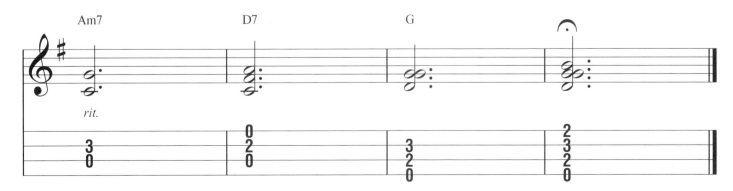

Spring, First Movement

from THE FOUR SEASONS
By Antonio Vivaldi

Moderately ♩ = 100

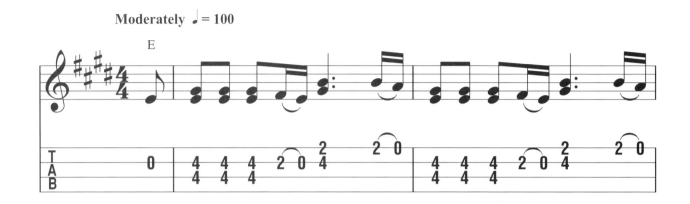

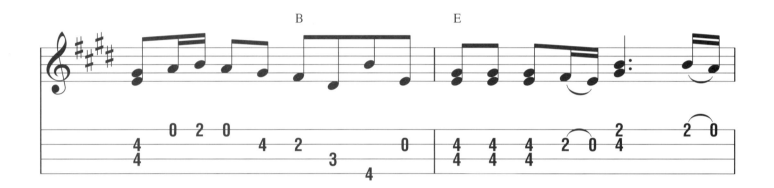

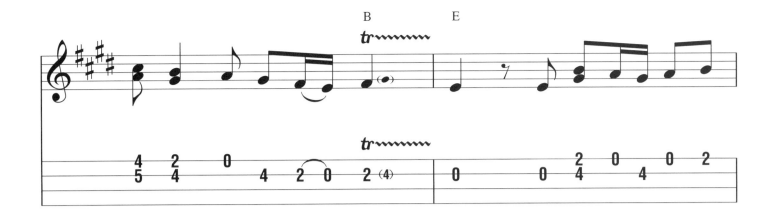

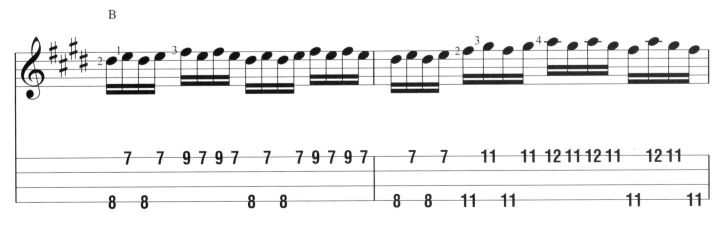

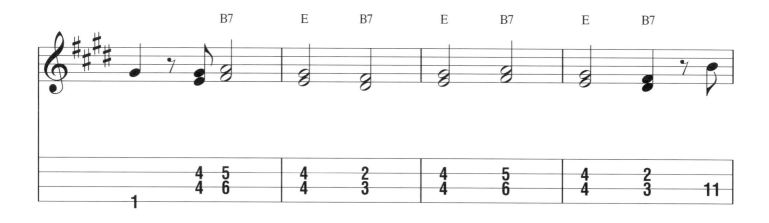

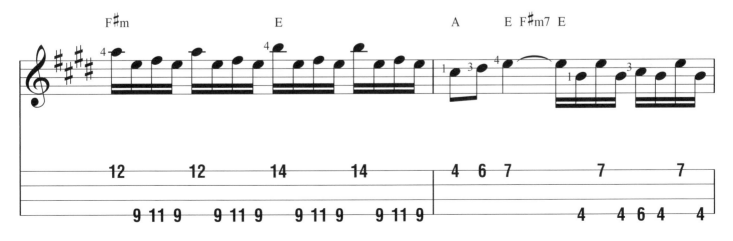

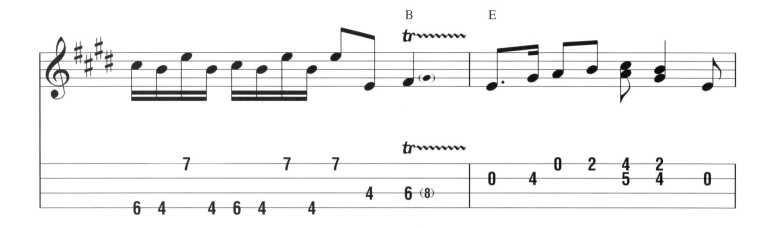

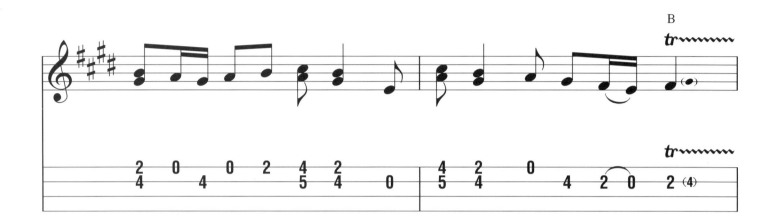

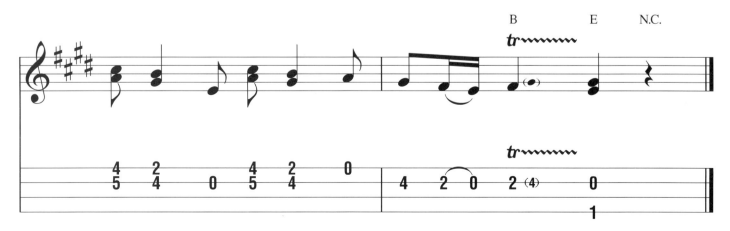

HAL•LEONARD UKULELE PLAY-ALONG

Now you can play your favorite songs on your uke with great-sounding backing tracks to help you sound like a bona fide pro! This series includes audio player tools, so you can adjust the tempo without changing the pitch and loop challenging parts.

1. POP HITS
00701451 Book/CD Pack........................$14.99

2. UKE CLASSICS
00701452 Book/CD Pack........................$12.99

3. HAWAIIAN FAVORITES
00701453 Book/CD Pack........................$12.99

4. CHILDREN'S SONGS
00701454 Book/CD Pack........................$12.99

5. CHRISTMAS SONGS
00701696 Book/CD Pack........................$12.99

6. LENNON & MCCARTNEY
00701723 Book/CD Pack........................$12.99

7. DISNEY FAVORITES
00701724 Book/CD Pack........................$12.99

8. CHART HITS
00701745 Book/CD Pack........................$14.99

9. THE SOUND OF MUSIC
00701784 Book/CD Pack........................$12.99

10. MOTOWN
00701964 Book/CD Pack........................$12.99

11. CHRISTMAS STRUMMING
00702458 Book/CD Pack........................$12.99

12. BLUEGRASS FAVORITES
00702584 Book/CD Pack........................$12.99

13. UKULELE SONGS
00702599 Book/CD Pack........................$12.99

14. JOHNNY CASH
00702615 Book/CD Pack........................$14.99

15. COUNTRY CLASSICS
00702834 Book/CD Pack........................$12.99

16. STANDARDS
00702835 Book/CD Pack........................$12.99

17. POP STANDARDS
00702836 Book/CD Pack........................$12.99

18. IRISH SONGS
00703086 Book/CD Pack........................$12.99

19. BLUES STANDARDS
00703087 Book/CD Pack........................$12.99

20. FOLK POP ROCK
00703088 Book/CD Pack........................$12.99

21. HAWAIIAN CLASSICS
00703097 Book/CD Pack........................$12.99

22. ISLAND SONGS
00703098 Book/CD Pack........................$12.99

23. TAYLOR SWIFT
00704106 Book/CD Pack........................$14.99

24. WINTER WONDERLAND
00101871 Book/CD Pack........................$12.99

25. GREEN DAY
00110398 Book/CD Pack........................$14.99

26. BOB MARLEY
00110399 Book/CD Pack........................$14.99

27. TIN PAN ALLEY
00116358 Book/CD Pack........................$12.99

28. STEVIE WONDER
00116736 Book/CD Pack........................$14.99

29. OVER THE RAINBOW & OTHER FAVORITES
00117076 Book/CD Pack........................$14.99

30. ACOUSTIC SONGS
00122336 Book/CD Pack........................$14.99

31. JASON MRAZ
00124166 Book/CD Pack........................$14.99

32. TOP DOWNLOADS
00127507 Book/CD Pack........................$14.99

34. CHRISTMAS HITS
00128602 Book/CD Pack........................$14.99

36. ELVIS PRESLEY HAWAII
00138199 Book/CD Pack........................$14.99

39. GYPSY JAZZ
00146559 Book/Online Audio....................$14.99

HAL•LEONARD® CORPORATION
7777 W. BLUEMOUND RD. P.O. BOX 13819 MILWAUKEE, WI 53213

www.halleonard.com

Prices, contents, and availability subject to change without notice.

Ride the Ukulele Wave!

The Beach Boys for Ukulele

This folio features 20 favorites, including: Barbara Ann • Be True to Your School • California Girls • Fun, Fun, Fun • God Only Knows • Good Vibrations • Help Me Rhonda • I Get Around • In My Room • Kokomo • Little Deuce Coupe • Sloop John B • Surfin' U.S.A. • Wouldn't It Be Nice • and more!

00701726 . . . . $14.99

Disney Songs for Ukulele

20 great Disney classics arranged for all uke players, including: Beauty and the Beast • Bibbidi-Bobbidi-Boo (The Magic Song) • Can You Feel the Love Tonight • Chim Chim Cher-ee • Heigh-Ho • It's a Small World • Some Day My Prince Will Come • We're All in This Together • When You Wish upon a Star • and more.

00701708 . . . . $14.99

Jack Johnson – Strum & Sing

Cherry Lane Music
Strum along with 41 Jack Johnson songs using this top-notch collection of chords and lyrics just for the uke! Includes: Better Together • Bubble Toes • Cocoon • Do You Remember • Flake • Fortunate Fool • Good People • Holes to Heaven • Taylor • Tomorrow Morning • and more.

02501702 . . . . $15.99

The Beatles for Ukulele

Ukulele players can strum, sing and pick along with 20 Beatles classics! Includes: All You Need Is Love • Eight Days a Week • Good Day Sunshine • Here, There and Everywhere • Let It Be • Love Me Do • Penny Lane • Yesterday • and more.

00700154 . . . . $16.99

Folk Songs for Ukulele

A great collection to take along to the campfire! 60 folk songs, including: Amazing Grace • Buffalo Gals • Camptown Races • For He's a Jolly Good Fellow • Good Night Ladies • Home on the Range • I've Been Working on the Railroad • Kumbaya • My Bonnie Lies over the Ocean • On Top of Old Smoky • Scarborough Fair • Swing Low, Sweet Chariot • Take Me Out to the Ball Game • Yankee Doodle • and more.

00696068 . . . . $12.99

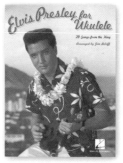

Elvis Presley for Ukulele

arr. Jim Beloff
20 classic hits from The King: All Shook Up • Blue Hawaii • Blue Suede Shoes • Can't Help Falling in Love • Don't • Heartbreak Hotel • Hound Dog • Jailhouse Rock • Love Me • Love Me Tender • Return to Sender • Suspicious Minds • Teddy Bear • and more.

00701004 . . . . $14.99

The Daily Ukulele

compiled and arranged by
Liz and Jim Beloff
Strum a different song everyday with easy arrangements of 365 of your favorite songs in one big songbook! Includes favorites by the Beatles, Beach Boys, and Bob Dylan, folk songs, pop songs, kids' songs, Christmas carols, and Broadway and Hollywood tunes, all with a spiral binding for ease of use.

00240356 . . . . $39.99

Glee

Music from the Fox Television Show for Ukulele
20 favorites for Gleeks to strum and sing, including: Bad Romance • Beautiful • Defying Gravity • Don't Stop Believin' • No Air • Proud Mary • Rehab • True Colors • and more.

00701722 . . . . $14.99

Jake Shimabukuro – Peace Love Ukulele

Deemed "the Hendrix of the ukulele," Hawaii native Jake Shimabukuro is a uke virtuoso. Our songbook features note-for-note transcriptions with ukulele tablature of Jake's masterful playing on all the CD tracks: Bohemian Rhapsody • Boy Meets Girl • Bring Your Adz • Hallelujah • Pianoforte 2010 • Variation on a Dance 2010 • and more, plus two bonus selections!

00702516 . . . . $19.99

The Daily Ukulele – Leap Year Edition

366 More Songs for Better Living
compiled and arranged by
Liz and Jim Beloff
An amazing second volume with 366 MORE songs for you to master each day of a leap year! Includes: Ain't No Sunshine • Calendar Girl • I Got You Babe • Lean on Me • Moondance • and many, many more.

00240681 . . . . $39.99

Hawaiian Songs for Ukulele

Over thirty songs from the state that made the ukulele famous, including: Beyond the Rainbow • Hanalei Moon • Ka-lu-a • Lovely Hula Girl • Mele Kalikimaka • One More Aloha • Sea Breeze • Tiny Bubbles • Waikiki • and more.

00696065 . . . . $9.99

Worship Songs for Ukulele

25 worship songs: Amazing Grace (My Chains are Gone) • Blessed Be Your Name • Enough • God of Wonders • Holy Is the Lord • How Great Is Our God • In Christ Alone • Love the Lord • Mighty to Save • Sing to the King • Step by Step • We Fall Down • and more.

00702546 . . . . $12.99

HAL•LEONARD® CORPORATION

7777 W. BLUEMOUND RD. P.O. BOX 13819 MILWAUKEE, WI 53213

Disney characters and artwork © Disney Enterprises, Inc.

Prices, contents, and availability subject to change.

1215